New Frontiers in Management Development

Edited by James L. Peters and Barbara H. Peters

Contents

From the President

Emerging global markets, dramatic worldwide political changes, and the impact of these forces on company cultures, pose exciting but difficult challenges to management development. Executives today, and certainly for the future, need to be quick on their feet and make decisions on matters without templates. They must be well-versed not only in their own functions, but in everything from Marketing to Human Resources to Manufacturing: And all on a worldwide scale.

Conventional development tracks for managers are just that—conventional. Creativity is lacking. In response to this need, The Conference Board held its Frontiers for Management Development Conference. It was a great success. Here now are the highlights from that conference.

On behalf of the Board, I wish to thank all the participants for their innovative ideas and fresh insights.

PRESTON TOWNLEY
President and CEO

Executive Summary

Economic globalization and an increasingly diverse work force are two of the major challenges confronting managers in the 1990s and beyond. As change unfolds worldwide, managers must develop creative and innovative strategies to successfully deal with tomorrow's business culture. The Conference Board held its Frontiers for Management Development Conference on April 25, 1990 to discuss cutting-edge theories and practices that address these issues. The following are highlights from the meeting.

The Globalization of Managers. "The playing field of the 1990s requires global managers," says David L. Dotlich, executive vice president, corporate relations, Bull HN Information Systems, Inc. "There is a new interdependence we have not seen before. Global managers must therefore develop a mindset that responds quickly to an increasingly integrated market and easily assimilates new ideas and innovation." The qualities and abilities of a global leader include flexibility, comfort with ambiguity, systemic thinking, team-orientation, cultural sensitivity, language skills, technology literacy, and vision.

Managing in the Era of the Knowledge Worker. Michael J. Ushka, director of information management, planning and program management, US Sprint, quotes Alvin Toffler to emphasize that business must make decisions that anticipate future needs. By the year 2000, the demands on workers will be vastly different he says: "The knowledge workers of 2000 will have characteristics of speed, quality and flexibility; they will have a broad background and be cross-trained and cross-functional. They will be comfortable with integrated global networks, thoroughly computer literate and will utilize computers as personal tools."

Leveraging Differences. "With 97 percent of today's management jobs held by white males, America is not capitalizing on its diversity," observes Donna Allen Taylor, valuing differences manager, Digital Equipment Corporation. "The melting pot syndrome has put people of difference in a blender. The lure of sameness blinds us to the oppression of homogeneity. We must move from a mindset that sees difference as problematic to one that views it as a competitive advantage. The ability to make a difference comes from people being different."

Managers as Leaders of Organizational Transformation. Organizations, like people, go through multiple developmental transformations. William R. Torbert, professor of management, Wallace E. Carroll School of Management, Boston College, views a capacity for self-restructuring as a transformation that is especially pertinent to globalization and rapid technological change. "A self-restructuring organization actively encourages developmental transformation experiences for its work teams, managers and business units." Research shows that American Managers don't exercise transforming power—a power that fosters empowerment and mutuality. Instead, they use the unilateral power of coercion, diplomacy or logistics.

Making Changes Happen: The Value of Partnerships. Reuben Mark, chairman, president and CEO, Colgate-Palmolive, says, "Colgate makes an enormous effort to partner with our suppliers, other companies and, most important, our own people." This philosophy of partnership is central to Colgate's program of change begun in 1983. "The business environment at that time was one of intense competition, slow growth, flat earnings, a stagnant stock price and takeover threats. To put building blocks in place for the 1990s, the agenda included focusing the company's business, establishing corporate goals and empowering its 27,000 people worldwide."

Building a Global Management Team. Motorola had been selling products worldwide for several decades when, in 1984, it recognized that it was a multinational company at best. "We had transferred competency outside the U.S.," admits A. William Wiggenhorn, corporate vice president and director of training and education. "Know-how resided in Israel, Malaysia and Germany—not in the U.S. And market growth was outside the U.S. as well." This realization led to the establishment of an executive development program that enables managers to understand the tools and techniques that make change happen and to continuously improve quality by benchmarking what others are doing. "To have market share, you must make these kinds of changes."

Management Development at Pepsi-Cola International. A PCI study identified on-the-job behaviors that make good managers. Success factors are: the ability to recruit, develop, manage and lead good people; the ownership of executive maturity, organizational savvy and technical knowledge; and the ability to communicate effectively and handle business complexity. "At Pepsi-Cola," states John R. Fulkerson, director of Human Resources, "classroom learning is of limited value; our people learn from challenging experiences. In developing the annual human resources plan for employees, the key question is, What experience do they need and where can they get it?"

Action Learning: Developing Strategic Leadership at TRW. Andrew J. Kaslow, director of management and organization development at TRW Automotive Sector, says, "Action learning is TRW's fast track to executive development." Defined as "a social process in which managers learn with and from each other by supportive attacks upon real and menacing problems," action learning focuses on the workplace, not the classroom. It is learner-oriented, not teacher-centered, and stresses real time over hypothetical leaning. Projects are emphasized, not research, and it practices intervention rather than simulation.

Creating Intrapreneurs. Carloyn D. Holt, senior consultant, Union Carbide Chemicals and Plastics Co., Inc., reported on successful intrapreneuring within the Specialty Chemicals division. "We were in a survival mode in the early 1980s. In addition to the competitive global marketplace, there were serious setbacks including the Bhopal tragedy and an attempted takeover. We restructured and emerged a smaller, highly leveraged firm. New business development became a high-priority goal and Innovation for Growth a core value. Through intrapreneuring, Specialty Chemicals created three new businesses in less than nine months."

Transforming Managers at Texaco. Richard C. Conant, manager, human resources development, and Hogan T. McWilliams, manager, training, spoke of Texaco's "crisis mode" in the mid- to late-1980s, just before it entered a transformative process. In five years, Texaco's work force went from 78,000 to 26,000. Facing the largest legal settlement ever imposed against a company, Texaco filed for Chapter 11 in 1987 to protect itself against disaster. Conant quoted Jim Kinnear, the new CEO, who said, "We are going to thrive, not just survive. Texaco is ours to build." Part of the building process was transforming management—with a focus on middle managers.

Managing Through Technological Transformations. "We stand at a crossroads with technology where we face major changes," began John Uzzi, vice president, Roy W. Walters & Associates. In order for businesses to create breakthrough opportunity they must undergo technological transformation. In such an organization (1) there is improved front-line staffing, (2) communication is fluid, (3) access to data and business information is easy, (4) technology is a corporate value, and (5) people investigate and experiment with leading-edge technology. "In a technological transformation, managers can align their energies, talents and skill in the direction of the future. They can work on the system, not in it. They can stop being a crisis intervener and start being a planner. The manager's job is to fuel the system and provide resources."

Assembly Line vs. Workstations. "In 1985, an assembly-line production environment prevailed at First Bank of Chicago. Nine people might have been involved in one letter of credit transaction," recalled Sheila Carvalho, vice president, Trade Finance. With so many people involved, the system was inefficient: revenues were declining, expenses were rising, and staff morale and productivity were low. The company underwent reorganization twice to ensure survival. Several lessons were learned: You must communicate and involve the staff from the beginning of the process, never emphasize productivity at the expense of quality, and focus on the customer while eliminating internal barriers to excellent customer service.

The Globalization of Managers

David L. Dotlich

Executive Vice President, Corporate Relations
Bull HN Information Systems, Inc.

We are all managing on a global playing field that requires new leaders. Today we see economic interdependencies that did not exist before—between companies, countries and continents. We see reduced tariff barriers and a marketplace open at all hours. Constant innovation and improvements can come from anywhere in the world at any time. In an environment where technology is virtually free, any company can gain a competitive advantage over another.

Global vs. International and Multinational Business

What is a global business and how does it differ from an international or multinational business? An international business is an organization structured around exports. Once your company has successfully competed in the domestic market, you begin to export products to other countries, to grow internationally.

A multinational business is a federation of independent national companies. Working at the corporate level of many multinational organizations, you deal with a general manager who oversees his "fiefdom." Developing a global strategy in this context is difficult because organizations have built distribution systems based on independent national companies. In multinational businesses today, team building occurs as ، companies try to trade off issues between distribution and worldwide strategy.

In a global corporation, the question is not where you do business but how you do it. It is not countries that define the organization but the process of doing business. The process is built around managing tradeoffs, such as human resources, capital, technology and production. At Bull, it would not be unusual, for example, to ask these sorts of questions if we were deciding whether to locate a R&D plant in Italy: What kinds of tax credits are gained there? What kinds of

skills do we have in Italy? How does this compare to investing in a similar facility in Massachusetts? In assigning global missions, the issue is always tradeoffs. A global manager must think in terms of the benefits and liabilities of any decision. There are no right or wrong answers. It is a matter of choosing among alternatives.

Global Companies: The New Model

A new paradigm has emerged in today's global companies. It is distinct from the model seen in the era of mass production industries, which focused on a scale of production that led to large hierarchies. Seven new characteristics are:

(1) A focus on continuous learning and adaptation; this becomes a key organizational value.

(2) A fluid, flat organizational structure.

(3) An ability to motivate and drive behavior through missions and visions rather than control.

(4) An emphasis on time-to-market, which is driven by the goal of return on investment.

(5) A use of human resources management systems that don't rely on extensive administrative processes and mechanisms since these divert time from quick customer response.

(6) A network of communications in which people talk laterally, rather than up and down the organization.

(7) Global thinking and local action, which means keeping an eye on the global strategy as you respond to local market requirements.

Globalization, Information Technology and Ideas

A global company tries to achieve linkages through information technology. Today, people believe that the driving force behind globalization is changes in world political structures. But the driving force is information technology. It literally wires the world. Through video text, for example, engineers can work together in different parts of a country in real-time to solve complex problems without ever meeting. Market improvements or innovations can be developed in one part of the world and become instantly available in another part.

A global company assigns a high value to invention, no matter where it occurs. In a hierarchical, industrial-age organization, the values said, "If it's not invented here, it's not useful to us." Today the values say, "No matter where it comes from, it probably has inherent value and we should use it." In the industrial age, we looked for economies of scale in the mass production cycle. Today's economies of scale refer to the number of ideas that a company can generate and move quickly around the world. Increasingly, we are managing ideas rather than products.

The information industry faces a tremendous shake-out today. The global playing field has room only for Olympic-class players. This accounts for the massive consolidation occurring worldwide. We are moving away from an ability to control the customer through proprietary information systems to an industry in which standards shape the operating environment; where one company's equipment must mesh with the next company's, systems integration becomes the norm, and the emphasis is on how to manage information.

Globalization and Human Resources Strategy

Developing leaders with a global mindset is difficult because many managers feel the need to control people, resources and money. This need to control is a barrier to functioning in a global environment. In a global company, shared information and the capacity to spread information becomes important.

What are the appropriate human resources strategies? Human resources has a different mission here than in a domestic or multinational company. The emphasis is on developing key values, exchanging people and using training as a lever to drive change in the company. Young people seeking global careers are valued. Performance management becomes critical and must be implemented on a worldwide basis. It is strategically important to develop a global human resources plan that defines business direction and strategy as well as skill profiles and career paths for people worldwide.

At Bull, we have instituted Relative Value Ranking. Last year, we conducted a worldwide study and found that 80 percent of our people were rated one or two on a scale of four. How do you get people to make distinctions about performance? If time-to-market, cycle time and improved performance are critical, how do you raise the bar? Our Relative Value Ranking "totem-poles" people—ranks them according to how they perform relative to everyone else. They can make career decisions based on what their managers tell them. This forces managers to make distinctions and to communicate these precisely.

We studied 165 managers in a global context to learn what their values were, what they desired from a global company and what they saw as important. At Bull, we discovered that all managers are concerned about management style in other countries. They fear that the French are too hierarchical, the Americans too informal, the Japanese too private. The study also suggested that there are common bases for knitting together a global company, such as a strong desire to be treated as an equal and to have a voice in projects that affect them. In short, there are ways to build a global organization based on common values among managers.

Global Leaders: Requirements and Development

Global companies need flexible leaders who can think in systemic terms and make tradeoffs in investments and people. In organizational development, systems thinking is critical. Because of the ability to do continuous prototyping of a company, organizational design will become a critical skill for global managers. You can create a computer simulation of what we call perpetual prototyping to assess whether the organization can achieve its goals. And you can factor in such variables as people's behavior. In the future, we will use this mechanism more and more. We also need leaders who understand global financial tradeoffs, such as taxation and producer-distributor pricing. We need people with language skills and technology literacy.

We develop managers and leaders at Bull in several ways. One is the International Management Program, a five-week course run in Europe, the U.S. and Japan. We train about 100 people annually and focus on global leadership skills. We challenge participants to learn and understand cross-cultural issues—Europe 1992, globalization, and what is happening in the Pacific Rim and elsewhere. We also conduct a two-week program for managers just below our top-level people. Here we emphasize such issues as the strategic direction of specific functions—marketing, finance and human resources. We assess the implications for different markets as these functions change.

Learning by Doing

It is critical to focus on functional and cross-functional team development. This means learning by doing. We no longer build teams by sending people to resorts to discuss how to work together. Organizational development is done in real-time. Facilitators are assigned to a joint R&D team, for example, where they work on a project, do a stop-action with the team, process what is happening in real-time and return to work.

Executive development must be tied to action learning. In our management programs, people are given real-time assignments; the CEO receives a report from each participant; and the report is immediately implemented. There are important implications for people's careers as a result of this course, not the least of which is the visibility they gain with the CEO.

Lessons for Global Management Development

What have we learned about developing managers for a global environment?

(1) Experiment with new organizational forms. Learn by doing because technology is moving rapidly in its capacity to organize and manage people.

(2) Emphasize key values.

(3) Respect local cultures in the context of key worldwide values.

(4) Move fast because time-to-market is the most critical aspect of the global market.

(5) Practice learning in real-time.

(6) Encourage managers to be comfortable with ambiguity.

(7) Manage human resources globally.

Global leadership strategies must be fast and efficient. They require visionaries at the top.

Managing in The Era of The Knowledge Worker

Michael J. Ushka
Director of Information Management,
Planning and Program Management
U.S. Sprint

Executives survey the chaos surrounding our businesses—rapidly changing technology, shifting markets, intense global competition—and often blame human resources for the mismatch between work force and corporate needs. The reality is that by the time executives convey their needs to human resources, it is often too late to prepare the work force for the challenge. Human resources must anticipate future needs and begin molding the work force accordingly.

Why does the future never seem to be what we predicted? Peter Drucker says, "Future planning has nothing to do with future decisions; it ensures the futurity of today's decisions." Forces at work today are producing a total transformation in the business climate, the economy, our organizations and the work force. Today's executives must understand and harness these forces to be prepared for the year 2000.

Yesterday's Knowledge Workers

In the 1980s, turbulence gripped the business community: the aftermath of the oil embargo; skyrocketing gold and silver prices and the near collapse of these markets; runaway inflation; and a 20-plus percent interest rate. These forces led some executives down the diversification path while others remained entrenched. Every firm focused on cost-saving and survival.

Knowledge workers of the early 1980s worked in traditional, hierarchical organizations with 12-17 layers of management. They probably had read Machiavelli's *The Prince* and Michael Maccoby's *The Gamesman*. They worked in the same department in the same firm in which they had started. They were loyal to the company and planned to stay until retirement. Their career paths were upward, through positions of increasing scope and responsibility in the same functional specialty. One day they hoped to head their departments. In other words, in the 1980s, it was one degree, one job, one department, one company and one purpose.

Their skills weren't related to their hands or backs but to their minds. They took information, applied reasoning and judgment—derived from education and experience—and rendered decisions to be carried out by others. Knowledge workers generally got their information from the nightly news, local newspapers and perhaps a journal or two. They pored over reports prepared by MIS departments and performed some manual analysis.

It is likely these knowledge workers had adding machines on their desks and, perhaps, personal calculators. Once satisfied that decisions were correct, they called for couriers to distribute the work or to return it to those who executed it. If knowledge workers of the early 1980s had any familiarity with computers, they most likely thought of them in terms of punch-cards and green-bar paper.

In the last decade, we have seen the aftermath of deregulation in the transportation, financial and telecommunications industries. An early recession followed by slow but steady expansion set us up for a double-whammy: (1) Record levels of borrowing in the public and private sectors transformed the U.S. from the world's largest creditor to the world's leading debtor economy. Fueled by junk bonds, we have seen feverish mergers and acquisitions. (2) The Japanese management miracle produced an influx of quality goods and services and threw every firm's survival into question.

Today's Knowledge Workers

Today, our knowledge workers' firms are likely to be focused on quality and productivity. Books like *Quality Is Free* and *A Passion for Excellence* are on their bookshelves, along with seminar notes on meeting management. While companies are still hierarchical, there is substantial flattening. Knowledge workers now spend considerable time on interfunctional task groups; many firms have become *ad hocracies*.

Typical knowledge workers have returned to school and earned MBAs. They also have 15-year-old BAs. They have left the department where they began and rotated in several departments, but not with the same company. They have worked in several firms, probably in several cities, and have developed a stronger commitment to their profession than to any firm. Knowledge workers' career paths are not as functional specialists; they are management generalists and technologists.

Knowledge workers stay on top of their business by using on-line services—Dow Jones, Dialog, Reuters, corporate clipping services, executive information systems and trade journals, most of them on electronic mail. They use PCs for decision-making, working with a variety of internal and external data. They use portable PCs while traveling, have a PC at home and carry an electronic pocket-diary to keep track of busy schedules. At the office, they plug their diaries into their PCs and upload their schedules. Communication is not by courier but by fax, electronic mail, cellular telephone and video conferencing. They are familiar with LANs, mice and probably use a mainframe.

Alvin Toffler tells us that the rate of change is increasing at an increasing rate. He says, "The year 2000 is destined to be as different [from today] as today is from 1910." In *Future Perfect*, Stanley Davis predicts a world where custom goods are available instantly, everywhere, at mass-market prices. He also predicts that the time-lag from product conception to delivery will shrink dramatically. For example, a factory-manufactured, custom-made house—to be assembled on the owner's property—will take 30-45 days from design to completion. The builder will produce 40,000 custom houses a year, compared to today's builder who takes at least 180 days to produce 400 homes.

The company of the future and its knowledge workers will focus on speed, quality and flexibility; they will compete in micromarkets with custom goods in real-time. Needs will be so complex that few specialists will remain. The hierarchy we see in today's organizations will be gone. Instead, cross-trained, cross-functional teams will assume the challenges. The fragmentation of markets across technologies, cultural groups, nations and regions will demand professionals with experience derived from tours in multiple functions, multiple companies, industries and nations.

Product managers, for example, may have engineering or physics degrees, marketing MBAs, and past assignments in finance, engineering, sales, information management and strategic planning. They may have experience in the energy, retailing, electronics and service industries. In general, tomorrow's knowledge workers will have graduate degrees.

Technology will facilitate more telecommuting as smart new systems that seek out events in real-time are deployed. These systems will match interest profiles run by neural networks and delivered in cellular multimedia formats that integrate image, voice and data. Expert systems will be common. They will function as personal assistants used in decision making, correlating, hypothesizing and synthesizing external and intern- al data. This will be facilitated by integrated worldwide networks accessing a global information base. Most computers will be embedded in common tools.

Preparing for 2000 and Beyond

How do we prepare knowledge workers for the year 2000? I offer three suggestions:

(1) *Learn how to learn*. Continuous change requires learning new things explicitly, not just implicitly. The future will be marked by lifelong learning at an accelerated pace. Those with superior learning skills will rise to the top.

(2) *Learn how to communicate and relate*. The instability of a multifunctional, multinational career places a premium on the ability to quickly establish rapport, gain loyalty, build trust and exact commitment.

(3) *Learn how to choose*. In the past, few decisions were required. We chose our college and major, picked a firm and stayed with it. In the year 2000, we will make more decisions in a week than our parents did in a lifetime.

Leveraging Differences

Donna Allen Taylor
Valuing Differences Manager
Manufacturing, Engineering and Marketing
Digital Equipment Corporation

America has profited from the melting pot. For many people it looked egalitarian and full of opportunity. Others saw it as a way of homogenizing cultural differences. Signaled by movements for Civil Rights, Black Power, Women and Gay Rights, many people who didn't fit the cultural mold began to stand up for their own models and standards, bridging American individualism on one side and a connection to their own roots on the other. An uneasy peace has emerged under which lie deep issues of disconnection.

The Dilemma of Differences

Many people today refuse to climb the corporate ladder by jumping into a blender. In other cases, the talents and competencies of people of difference have been churned up beyond recognition in a blender. This problem, combined with changing demographics, thrusts business on the horns of a dilemma.

This dilemma can push business to the threshold of the most potent antidote for the constriction of innovation, productivity and creativity yet available to us. There are strategies we can employ to face this situation. One option is particularly ripe for harvest. Two other options are used consciously or unconsciously by many businesses every day. I make note of the latter because the challenge I put forth is about choice. Whether your company takes direct action or not, you make choices each day.

Options for Workplace Diversity

Option One: We will choose based on similarity, likeness, comfort and predictability. Then our challenge as a company or business is to sift out true similarity from a decreasing number of talented people.

Option Two: We will meet our compliance requirements—EEO and Affirmative Action. It is costly for us to lose contracts if we aren't in compliance. Once they are hired, it is up to them whether they sink or swim, although we will implement some programs to help.

Option Three: We will make an organizational commitment to understand, value and leverage our diversity because it is smart business. Peter Drucker argues that this is a major evolution in organizations. It is a movement from the 1925 version of the organization, a command and control organization, to one that more closely resembles a symphony orchestra.

I use the terms leveraging differences and leveraging diversity to advocate something different from the pluralism that exists today. The point is not that we control our diversity but that we unleash it, that we leverage the power of diversity, that we put it to full and positive use as one of the underpinnings of corporate success.

How will managers guide, motivate, teach and learn from people who do not share their cultural norms and assumptions? How will employees work effectively with colleagues who remind them of people they have not trusted in the past? How do we move employees from the experience of being controlled or devalued to an experience of empowerment and participation? Failure to use the skills and potential of employees may not be their fault alone. We may share the blame.

A Valuing Differences Strategy

Leveraging diversity requires innovative thinking, pioneering efforts and pervasive dedication. This is not a management training course. Digital Equipment Corporation has been dedicated to a valuing differences strategy since the 1970s. The work evolved from a discovery that traditional EEO work reinforced an "us-them" mentality and didn't encourage white males, women and minorities to build relationships.

Four years ago, we established positions for valuing differences managers in the three major parts of the corporation. Today many people participate in valuing differences work at many levels. One manufacturing engineering site developed "celebrating differences" events to raise awareness of the differences at work in a particular site and to reinforce the notion that it is important to recognize and value differences. This idea spread.

In the sales and services group, three human resources employees developed an introductory workshop, Understanding the Dynamics of Difference, that was refined and sent on to management development. Today it is the most popular workshop in management education. We keep the work of EEO and Valuing Differences separate to reinforce our belief that these are different efforts with different goals, skills and methodologies.

Lessons Already Learned

These are lessons Digital Equipment Corporation has learned:

(1) Activities are important to stir the pot but they don't create systemic change. This work is about systemic change.

(2) Specialists who lead and deliver this work need to be like heads of posses. Often people who lead differences work are hired like the gunslingers in old Western movies. To bring in hired guns, charge them to clean up the town, and then let them ride off into the sunset is dangerous business. Preferably, engage someone who actually lives in the town, someone you know, someone who can head up a posse of townspeople. If this work doesn't have the organization's total involvement and isn't seen as vital to the company, you will be wasting your time and money.

(3) Valuing differences is pioneering work. Keep it a distinct function or department so that you don't blur what it is about. Position it properly.

The following elements comprise the design to move work environments to a place of leveraging diversity:

- *Personal awareness work.* This enables people to ask questions about their assumptions and experiences of difference and sameness.
- *Knowledge building.* This includes workshops, seminars and meetings to increase knowledge about hidden differences, such as differences in thinking and problem-solving preferences, as well as the more overt differences like gender, culture, race and class.

- *Skill development.* Possessing knowledge and awareness doesn't mean that you own the skills. You must be able to influence and impact. If we don't speak the same language, how do we come to common points of communication?
- *Organizational assessment.* They are responsible for exploring and analyzing the infrastructure, rules, policies, regulations, business norms, behavioral norms, the job selection process, the development processes—all the structural underpinnings that support heterogeneity and suppress homogeneity or do the opposite.
- *Goal setting.* This involves performance, feedback and reward mechanisms to support an organizational move toward leveraging differences. You need clear goals, rationales and accountability, and you must provide people with the necessary tools.

A Differences Strategy and EEO/Affirmative Action

What about the role of EEO and Affirmative Action? Complying with regulations, getting contracts, setting goals, tracking the presence of diversity, and enforcing rules and regulations about harassment and discrimination are all part of this work. Over 30 countries have enacted such legislation and they are not about to stop looking over companies' shoulders, nor should they. Digital hasn't lost its need for a strong internal EEO department. The data it provides tells us how far the company has to go.

If you think about the visible differences—the differences we track with EEO data—some things remain largely unchanged in U.S. business. In corporations, for example, 97 percent of senior management positions are still held by white males. For women, the largest group of difference within American business, many studies show that managers consistently rate women's performances lower than men's even though the performances are the same. Men get higher pay raises even if their performances are rated equal. Men's voices are listened to while women's are often dismissed by both men and women. If you don't have a top-notch EEO/Affirmative Action department staffed by some of your best people, you are courting disaster by denying yourselves a barometer of what happens to differences of all kinds.

While leveraging diversity work seeks to build a new paradigm about differences, it must partner with other technologies in human resources—whether it is EEO, management development or employee relations—to ensure that they are working toward a common environmental goal.

In his book *More Like Us*, James Fallows asks organizations how large their radius of trust is. I think of the radius of trust as a circle. Inside the circle is "us" and outside the circle is "them," and we don't have to be fair or listen to "them." Ask yourself what the differences are within and outside your radius of trust and how this impacts your organization's success.

Valuing differences impacts your company's mindset about diversity. This work seeks to move from a mindset that sees differences as problematic to one that sees differences as a competitive advantage, whether these are differences of style, gender or culture. The challenge is to create an environment in which each employee contributes to his or her fullest ability. Recognize that a big part of each person's ability to make a difference comes from his or her being different. Affirmative Action gets people in the door. Good management helps people become sound managers of people and processes. Leveraging diversity enlarges the radius of trust and enables managers to recognize and utilize what each person contributes. This creates a better connection between effort and recognition.

Preparing for Long-Term Organizational Change

Option three—to understand, value and leverage diversity—commits a company to a long-term process of organizational change. If you choose it, you should:

(1) Develop and communicate an overarching business reason for doing it.

(2) Develop and convey a picture of the desired end-state—what it will look and feel like to work in this kind of company once you get there.

(3) Clarify what you mean by differences, pluralism and diversity. Are you talking about protected classes, about the full range of differences? Is this something for "them" or for all of "us"?

(4) Acquire or create the skilled resources you need to launch and drive a quality systemic intervention.

(5) Ensure that the basic architecture of the work includes awareness, knowledge, skill-building, organizational scanning of processes and norms, and a commitment to fix those processes and norms that inhibit achieving your goals.

(6) Make it okay for a manager to try something different, to test a new approach, to pilot a new intervention. This is leading-edge work. It must be okay to slip off the edge and then get back on again.

(7) Celebrate the new model's heroes, heroines and teams who exemplify the end-state or progress toward it.

(8) Hold all people accountable for their behavior and efforts as work progresses.

(9) Partner with existing human resources and managerial work.

(10) Develop a way to measure what you are doing. All efforts must be made with a view toward expanding the radius of trust.

The lure of sameness—the ease of speaking to someone who shares your language, the predictability achieved in choosing people who think just like you—blinds us to the oppression of homogeneity. The challenge of understanding, valuing and leveraging diversity is a challenge to unleash all our capabilities for excellence.

This is the smartest option for anyone doing business in the U.S., a nation built on diversity. But it means we must do things differently and must act now rather than later. The U.S. is favorably positioned to combine the rugged individualism for which we are famous with our ability to cooperate. In some cases, we have lost the fulcrum that creates the balance between these two. Leveraging diversity is the fulcrum in the workplace. The richness of our diversity is our strength, if only we can learn to harness it. The choice is ours.

Managers as Leaders of Organizational Transformation

William R. Torbert

Professor of Management
Wallace E. Carroll School of Management
Boston College

The theory from which I work attempts to take development seriously for the first time. Articulated by Jean Piaget in Switzerland in the 1930s, the theory asserts that individuals go through multiple stages of development. Each stage is a fundamental transformation in which people completely reorganize the world for themselves. Piaget traced these changes in children who always seem to be changing into someone unrecognizable. Adults can and ought to do this, but they rarely do because our educational and business organizations do not help people develop.

Transformations in Individuals and Organizations

Not only are there multiple transformations in individuals but also in organizations. Every successful organization, and each successful project within an organization, consists of multiple transformations. Managers are needed, therefore, who are capable of leading multiple reframings, usually in periods of great turbulence. The problem here is that the theory also tells us that only a manager or organization at a late stage of development welcomes these transformations. Today, it is not likely that there are many managers or organizations in these late stages.

Are today's managers equipped to meet the challenge of transformation? The answer is simple: No. What are the challenges of leading project teams and whole organizations through multiple transformations? First, there is no one-shot solution. A business needs to be shaken up not once but repeatedly. But there is a more fundamental issue here. Transformation is not a problem; yet we see ourselves as problem-solvers. A problem is convergent. You must define it and solve it.

A transformation is divergent. And this requires a change in our frame of thinking, in our assumptions.

Transformation and Power

The other problem, which is a serious one, is that transformation cannot be created by applying unilateral power. Direct force, the application of resources, diplomacy, logistics, clear plans and rationale: None of these will generate transformation. But these are the familiar ways we use power.

Transforming power is fundamentally different and requires an awareness of what is actually going on—not your version or vision of it. Paradoxically, it involves mutuality. The mother hen cannot get the egg to hatch simply by breaking the shell. The hen must align with the chick inside who seeks to get out. If it is not mutual, the chick inside will die. There must be constant mutuality among your organization's members.

Transforming power generates empowerment and creates a wider world-view for the organization. It doesn't hoard power; rather it disperses it; and it is open to challenge. Transforming power is operative only when all the power sources are themselves open to challenge. This is a threatening process. When our own frame is at stake, the heat is difficult to endure.

Stages of Transformation

What are the predictable transformations managers experience before they reach the point where they can exercise organizational power? Managers may still be at the first stage of development, the Opportunist stage, in both positive and negative ways. The Opportunist typically exploits force. A child normally reaches this stage at eight-years-old. It can be profitable to employ a salesperson who is at the Opportunist stage—if the individual is well managed.

It can be useful to have a manager at the Diplomat stage also—an age-12 development—particularly when you are concerned with meeting peer group definitions of proper behavior. Characteristically, diplomats try to gain favor by integrating everybody's agenda. Indeed, they can be the glue for the organization. But diplomats are so loyal to existing norms that they are not interested in change. Many people enter the work force at these early stages and there is no rule that an individual will ever experience a transformation.

At the Technician stage, the next level, there is an exercise of logistics. The Achiever stage, which follows, is characterized by people who work well with all three types of power—unilateral force, diplomacy, and logistics. Achievers are flexible and, therefore, useful for managing. Only in the later stages, when Strategists and Magicians emerge, do people begin to conceive and actually exercise transforming power. At the Strategist stage, it is focused on advocating transforming power—helping others transform—not on achieving self-transformation.

Opportunists and Diplomats in the Work Force

How many managers do you find in the different stages? It varies by position in the hierarchy—the higher up the ladder, the fewer people in the early stages. In a sample study of 500 people at different management levels, we found that 6 percent are Opportunists. Opportunists can kill an organization, even if there are few of them, because they are jungle fighters, totally reject feedback and hold their cards close to the vest. They are deceptive, manipulative, have fragile self-control, externalize blame and take advantage of superiors who are diplomats—because diplomats don't want to offend anybody.

Diplomats number about 12 percent in our sample, mainly at the lower levels. They provide organizational glue because they follow orders well, prefer routine work, avoid conflict, save face and are self-subordinating yes-people.

Technicians and Achievers as Managers

At the Technician stage, you begin to see most of the work force—many managers, even vice presidents and CEOs. Technicians are problem-solvers. They seek to stand out through the excellence of their performance; their concern is always with efficiency over effectiveness; they look for causes; they are analytical, dogmatic and argumentative; they own the right frame and logic. They change only if their logic tells them to change.

They are perfectionists and wonderful subordinates because they see every detail. But they will accept feedback only about their craft and only from craft masters. Many people in business work this way.

Many managers are in the Achiever stage. Yet this is the first stage where a person actually manages. Achievers strive for excellence but, for the first time, respect differences, welcome feedback about their behavior and appreciate complexity. They are not sold on a single logic, are interested in being effective rather than just efficient, are results-oriented, have long-term goals and initiative.

The problem here is that top executives are meant to be more than Achievers. Top managers must set goals, not just achieve them. They must develop long-term strategies, create coherent units out of diversity and model learning-in-action. Achievers are occasionally willing to learn about changing their behavior but not about changing their frame. Achievers don't realize they are operating in a frame that is simply one of many frames. Few corporate vice presidents have transformed beyond the Achiever stage.

Strategists as Leaders

Among senior executives, only 14 percent are Strategists. Even with senior executives, the largest group is at the Technician stage. But Strategists and still later stage executives are the ones most likely to lead organizational transformation. You need Strategists because this is the first stage where people see uniqueness, see the rare moments when a company can seize historical or market niches.

Strategists, who are essential in a global environment, value continuous learning. Strategists are aware of paradox, are willing to assume many roles, and are oriented affirmatively to the political process. Strategists realize that the creation of a shared frame among multiple frames is necessary and can be a positive process. They are concerned with creative conflict resolution, which is necessary to negotiate among frames.

What does all this have to do with the bottom line? In a small study done by John Hirsch of Boston University with 13 ophthalmologists, the average 1987 gross business revenues of these entrepreneurial doctors was $330,000 for the Technicians; $1,200,000 for the Achievers; and $4,200,000 for the Strategists. The lowest annual revenue for each stage is more than three times as great as the highest annual revenue for the preceding stage.

Why are there such dramatic differences in business outcomes in the various stages? Technicians insist on doing everything themselves; they don't trust anyone to do the work properly. Achievers realize they have an office staff to use and coordinate; they know they can get good results from people and retain them longer by delegating all the technical work. The Strategists not only have learned how to use a staff but also how to build partnerships. They run multisite businesses.

Magicians and Transformation

The problem remains, however, that we still haven't discussed a manager who can exercise transforming power. Only the Magicians use this power. The Magician relies on the power of authenticity, including the possibility of being authentically wrong. They change when change is indicated. They are willing to engage in continuous experiential inquiry whatever the setting. Few American managers exercise transforming power and this is why we aren't ready to meet the transformation challenge.

But there is some good news. There are leaders who have exhibited transforming power in the Magician stage. Lee Iacocca may be at the Magician stage. If he can transform Chrysler Corporation a second time, it will suggest that he has achieved the level of authenticity exhibited in Chrysler's first transformation.

Other Magicians include: Jean Riboud, an extraordinarily paradoxical man who was a socialist but led one of the best companies in the world; the Motorola executive team; Red Auerbach, who was one of the only managers in history to create three excellent dynasties; and Lech Walesa, who led Solidarity, the most exciting political movement in history; never has there been a more mutual movement.

Pope John XXIII, CEO of the largest organization in the world, led a peaceful transformation of his organization from an inward-looking to an outward-looking, global one. Early in his reign, Pope John XXIII provided an inspiring lesson by appointing his opponent—who had exiled John from Italy for 30 years—Secretary of State. By seating his greatest enemy right next to him, the Vatican II Council became a true dialogue of differences.

What can we do, even though we are not transformational leaders, to create and encourage transformation? Recognize in a mission statement that qualitative development, in addition to quantitative growth, is essential to an organization in the next decade. Make each member of the team a leader. There is no better way to teach leadership than to practice it. There is room in any task force of six or seven members for each to play a different leadership role. To make this work, you need performance feedback. You will never achieve performance excellence unless you structure feedback into the ongoing work.

This is risky and explosive work but the positive results far outweigh the negative ones. Even the negatives have important lessons for us. You must constantly structure challenging developmental opportunities for which managers can volunteer; move managers across functions; and create trial leadership roles that run for short periods.

Making Changes Happen: The Value of Partnerships

Reuben Mark

Chairman, President and Chief Executive Officer
Colgate-Palmolive Company

Colgate-Palmolive Company devotes a great deal of effort to partnerships—with outside companies, with joint ventures worldwide, with our advertising agencies and with our suppliers. The most important partnerships, however, are with our own employees, the 27,000 Colgate people worldwide. Colgate is truly a global company with factories and full installations on the ground in 62 countries; our products are sold in over 160 countries.

Deciding to Change

In the early 1980s, Colgate had to change or face declining profitability with all the possible consequences. We experienced intense competition, slow growth in our core business categories, flat earnings, a stagnant stock price, and a significant takeover threat because of our undervaluation in the the marketplace. More critical, perhaps, was the company culture—what people thought about each other and what we thought about them. The culture was family-oriented. Everyone had grown up in the company.

At the same time, there was a tolerant attitude about less than optimal performance standards, and this affected how we rewarded and compensated our people. We had an automatic compensation system in which regular increases prevailed despite performance. The world was changing, however. We had to change too.

Developing and Implementing the Plan for Change

In 1984, we developed and began to implement an eight-year plan. The first key objective was to focus the company. Colgate had become a conglomerate because management had lost faith in the basic business. We

owned food companies, sports companies, and a health care company. The basic business was milked to pay for companies we didn't know how to manage. To help focus Colgate, we sold 38 entities; we closed or reconfigured 32 of 100 factories; and we took major write-offs. Through divestment and elimination of many layers, we reduced our employees from 43,000 to 27,000. The plan also included specific goals for financial performance, stock market and shareholder value, and cash flow. It also included many soft notions: We must change our motivation systems; we must press decision making down; we must foster an entrepreneurial spirit. These hard and soft corporate initiatives were the backbone of a plan we promulgated worldwide. We set high goals. Today we are above levels that five years ago we thought impossible to reach.

Empowering people is the essence of change in any organization. This process is uncomfortable for most managers because people who move up the corporate ladder have been assertive line managers accustomed to exerting control. To relinquish this control is extraordinarily difficult. You must motivate people to buy into this, own it, and move ahead on their own initiative.

Linking Compensation to Performance

Key imperatives in the partnership process are to link compensation directly to individual, group and corporate performance, and to encourage innovation and entrepreneurial behavior. The difficulty is in the implementation. You must build a global team, continuously strengthen the global organization, and develop a creative response to changing work force needs.

We used to administer uniform compensation. Whether we had a great year or a poor one, I would receive a 6 percent bonus. Motivational factors here are small. At the senior level, therefore, we linked pay with performance. Today, this practice has spread throughout the organization, including the support and clerical staff. Today, if your division had a good year, you may do very well, or you may be penalized if the company didn't perform well. Staff people, R&D and engineering, for example, are tied to their group's specific performance as well as corporate performance. This policy is working well. It is a flexible tool that, as you move along a long-term plan, reveals those areas that need work.

In addition to direct compensation, we make a major effort to share stock with employees. Previously, the only employees who received stock were senior managers. Now there is an effort to distribute stock, in the form of direct grants and options, to every employee worldwide. We want all our people to be sensitive to Colgate stock because our objective is to build shareholder value.

Encouraging Innovation and Entrepreneurial Behavior

We restructured the organization worldwide and eliminated several layers to get decision making closer to the marketplace and closer to Colgate's employees. We broadened spans of control to get more involvement. This is a difficult idea for some people. We had to change some of our management team to ensure that this worked. We now run many employee recognition programs. We want each employee worldwide to feel that he or she is valued and can make a difference at Colgate. All this requires careful management.

One program, called the *Chairman's You Can Make a Difference*, is a worldwide, mandatory effort. If you are a factory worker, for example, with an idea about how to improve the line or to achieve better quality, you can be nominated for a local award, either by yourself, your peers or your supervisor. Quarterly, a local committee decides who will receive the awards. The worldwide winners, and their spouses, travel to New York for our annual meeting where they are introduced to shareholders. The purpose of these programs is to formally ask for ideas, and then to formally acknowledge and reward them.

Building a Global Team

The key element in building a global team is communication. It is important to tell the same story to all of our global employees. You can have only one set of goals and initiatives and everyone must know them. Colgate has a series of in-house videotapes on marketing,

manufacturing and global issues, among other topics, that employees are encouraged to view. Each quarter, there is a Colgate World Report video tape that reviews what we are doing. These tapes are used in sessions in New York with the top 100 people who, in turn, use them in meetings with their people, who then use them in meetings with their people. This is one way to ensure that people at all levels worldwide are exposed to the same ideas and information.

Also, we work to continuously strengthen the global organization. People begin at Colgate today knowing that they will be global; knowing that they will travel overseas as part of their training and in subsequent assignments. This is agreed to in advance. We therefore attract people who wish to spend part or all of their careers abroad.

But we have broken with Colgate's tradition of only promoting from within to fill gaps. We have improved considerably the quality of our management group as a result. Vitally important is our recruitment of minorities and women. We have four geographic divisions, and I was determined to see a woman as president of one of them. There was no internal candidate; we went outside and specifically recruited a very senior woman to be president. More of this specifically targeted activity must occur because it will not happen by osmosis.

Responding Creatively to the Changing Work Force

We try to be responsive to the human needs of our people. If we truly are a team, we must worry about this critical aspect. The top people in the company must be involved with human issues. If the top people are not pushing and pressuring, it just doesn't happen. At Colgate, we have established a flexible benefits package and several cutting-edge programs, such as helping people with mortgages and refinancing existing mortgages.

These are the building blocks to take us through the 1990s—our partnerships with people will make it happen. The critical lessons we have learned are: (1) You must push hard on these issues. Simply talking about them won't work; and (2) Leadership must change or be changed. In this process, you encounter people who are trying but they just can't change their views on these issues. As well-intentioned as they are, they must change or be removed from the organization.

It is astounding what an organization can accomplish once it becomes dedicated to change. Goals that seemed impossible become possible. But everyone must be motivated to continue reaching and stretching. Your continuous communication to your total organization will be vital in this effort.

Building a Global Management Team

A. William Wiggenhorn

Corporate Vice President & Director of
Training and Education
Motorola, Inc.

At Motorola in 1984, there were two schools of thought worldwide. One advocated installing barbed wire around North America and simply "bombing competitors out of the sky" if they tried to climb into the heartland market. The other school advocated changing the way we operated—to go where the markets existed and where they were emerging. This distinction is important because we already had 24 percent of our people in Asia, 14 percent in Europe and 12 percent in other parts of the world. We had been doing business outside the U.S. for 25-30 years. It became clear that if we were to survive and maintain market share, we had to compete *globally*.

For Motorola, it was also the beginning of a realization that, for over 20 years, we had *transferred competency outside* the U.S.. If we planned to build a certain type of factory, for example, we had to import know-how that resided in other countries, such as Malaysia, Singapore and Israel. When we examined future market growth, we saw that it would be outside the U.S. We had to go after that market.

Transformation Begins: An Executive Program

Transformation at Motorola began in 1984 with a senior executive program. The CEO, who heads the program, selects an annual topic, brings together the top 200 executives from around the globe to discuss the issue, and, following the symposium, initiates action. This program, which is mandatory, has become a strong catalyst for change.

Since 1984, the basic theme has been *quality*: quality of service, administration and people. Quality is increasingly important as we better understand the

global game and appreciate customer expectations worldwide. In 1986, when we focused on customer satisfaction, we defined it as "*meeting* customer expectations." By the end of 1987, we changed the definition to "*exceeding* customer expectations." Now we *anticipate* the needs of the customer. This means you get close to the customer, not just other managers.

The result is an appreciation of the tools and techniques needed by the work force to make change happen. Many American executives insist, for example, that English is the language of global business; so they do all their training in English and encourage the 40 percent who don't speak English to learn it. But if you want tools and techniques to be used by the entire work force, you must translate them into other languages to ensure that they are seen as positive. In 1984, for example, our executives wanted to deal with productivity. When you translate productivity into the languages with which we work, it can be a negative word. *Quality*, on the other hand, is a positive word when translated. Quality is acceptable to Malaysians; productivity reminds them of colonialism. So you must be genuinely sensitive to language.

Executives Focus on Asia

Asia was the topic selected for the senior executive program in 1984: Asia's past, present and future; country by country; company by company. We learned, for instance, that Goldstar was not an Alabama firm but an aggressive Korean company that had probably achieved more in 15 years than Motorola had in 25; that NEC had more people studying U.S. culture, language, idioms and customs than the U.S. State Department was preparing for the Foreign Service. We had to alter our world stereotypes. Many Motorola executives thought that India was a poor country; we learned, however, that middle-class Asian Indians outnumbered the entire population of the United Kingdom. Motorola knew it had to change management perceptions and behavior by looking closely at today's world.

We have made mistakes. After this symposium, for example, everybody set forth to capture the Asian market. A headline in a Taiwanese newspaper read, "Motorola to Hire 50,000 People." That was a shock. What had happened was every division and group manager spoke with the Taiwanese Minister of Labor about the future of his division or group in Taiwan. The Minister simply added up all the employees in the various divisions discussed. So we learned to move toward a *country* focus.

Lessons on Cycles, Customers, Communication

We also learned that our cycle time was too long, especially for decision making. In the past, we worked through many levels of bureaucracy. To compete globally, we work on a shortened decision-making cycle and we get back to people more quickly. Now we are discussing not one but four corporate influence centers: in London, Chicago, Tokyo and Singapore. These could be four Motorola entities capable of speaking for the entire company.

The journey from 1984 to 1989 is dramatic. We didn't get customer satisfaction right in 1988 so we did remedial customer satisfaction training in 1989. We were accustomed to telling markets what they wanted. But today's customers are more sophisticated and know what they want. We needed to change our mentality—to listen to buyers worldwide, not just in the U.S.

We received interesting and useful feedback. First, people told us our products were terrific. Doing business with us was difficult, however, and we lacked personality. Customers expected to deal with a person, not a company. This was a strong message, particularly from Asians and Europeans. We learned that to develop the business, senior employees had to visit the accounts. Senior people didn't know how to communicate on sales calls, however, especially in different cultures. Much of our training now focuses on the critical component of communication.

Components in the Long-Range Plan

One important outcome of this process is that Motorola developed a long-range plan. We established a 20-year goal to find people who are the "best in class." Our beliefs play a key part here. One of our beliefs is a respect for people. Another is uncompromising integrity and ethics. We are implementing ethics training

on a large-scale, and have developed multiple models for the training. Part of this includes a dialogue to determine what it means to do business in a particular culture. We try to learn how other people think so that we can understand what integrity and ethics mean in different societies.

Six Sigma is our definition of quality; it means you are entitled to three errors for every one million opportunities. Cycle time covers the time from the customers' expression of need to the moment they happily pay you. Product and manufacturing leadership means that it is okay to get on a plane and travel to do business; that it is okay to send a few additional words over a fax to be friendly. Profit improvement becomes a means to achievement not the end in itself. Cooperation between organizations is a new value and a change. Before, we advocated participative management within the operating unit; today, we insist on cooperation between organizations and between cultural groups.

Executive Programs Stimulate Action

We took these actions, among others, as a result of the senior executive symposiums:

(1) We formed a task force on Asia. We took the best people away from their jobs full-time. In the past, task force members remained on their regular jobs as well. And, typically, they were not top-level people.

(2) We created an international office to present one face to the customer.

(3) We started to rethink offshore manufacturing. We are there to penetrate markets—not to obtain cheap labor—to take our design to the marketplace and to begin to study other markets in depth.

(4) We ran study sessions with our top 30 people. These two-day, ongoing programs examine different cultures, explore their business practices and measurement systems, and invite guests from host countries to describe Motorola's image in their society.

(5) We assembled teams of people from the study groups to penetrate specific markets. These teams receive one to two weeks of cultural training before entering the market. Training incorporates the culture of the specific country as well as the Motorola culture.

The Changes Driving Globalization

Some efforts we have made to drive the global process are:

Defining what Motorola means. You cannot buy anyone else's definition. The factory of the future has a specific meaning for us as well as quality and cycle time. Concepts must be defined so that they can be translated worldwide in the language of employees and customers.

Pushing change through multinational teamwork. You also need a champion who is willing to give much of his or her life. Usually, it is a former general manager who has a tough reputation and is accustomed to a large staff. Give this person a staff of one and the assignment to push the concept through teamwork until it is institutionalized in the organization worldwide.

Educating from the top down. The language issue is an example. We all speak English in Chicago, but the equipment we buy is made in Japan, Korea, Israel and Germany. If we only speak English, we are able to understand only those product features that our suppliers choose to translate for us. This can lead to costly mistakes. We now offer considerable language training, particularly in Japanese, German, French, and Mandarin. Beginning at the top, implement unit by unit to ensure rapid success.

Changing the metrics. The measurement system should actually drive what you want to achieve. Today most of the measurement at Motorola is of quality and cycle time. Common measurements across the organization allow our 104,000 people to speak to each other.

Motorola in Japan

Motorola has been in Japan for more than 20 years. We knew we had to succeed there, so we assembled a team. The American and Japanese team is engaged in a process in which they explore the strengths of each group, to achieve the best of each. We agreed to certain concepts: accountability, teamwork, performance orientation, loyalty, discipline, explicit reward, strong and formal relationships, flexibility, experience, diversity, professional orientation and a long-term horizon. The general manager of Nippon Motorola spends at least 50 percent of his time managing these issues.

Out of this process certain tasks were identified:

(1) Develop a common vision that all partners can share. Meetings must be conducted in Japanese and translated into English. The set of values must be the organization's, not American or Japanese.

(2) Develop a common system and a clear understanding of its strategic role and then foster a shared perception of this role in Japan and the U.S.

(3) Foster formal and informal communication.

(4) Build stability.

(5) Engage in total team-building from top to bottom.

Today, we are moving teams between countries to learn from each other. Study assignments run from one to three years. Any team that is assigned to Japan receives eight days of language training for every two weeks of the tour. In our semiconductor group, we have moved U.S. production teams to Japan for one month to observe how their Japanese counterparts perform their jobs. For this exchange, we have found employees don't need common languages since they build their own communication. This process is costly but the returns have been extraordinary.

We have recently hired cultural anthropologists from America and Japan. They are preparing for a one-year assignment. We are teaching them everything we can about the environments at Motorola and Nippon Motorola. Their assignment: to assist Motorola's efforts to become a global organization.

Managing Through Technological Transformations

John Uzzi
Vice President
Roy W. Walters & Associates

We stand at a crossroads with technology where we face major choices. One option uses technology to follow the routinization route, automating work into many fine pieces and creating dull jobs that almost run themselves—where people essentially serve the machine. This approach has some attractive elements. With the recruitment problems companies are experiencing—not finding people with basic abilities in math and reading, for example—it simplifies work so much that it is difficult to make a mess.

But this approach misses the major opportunity that technology offers. Technology provides power to people by giving them access to information and enhancing their ability to perform key job functions. It also allows us to create more challenging jobs. To accomplish this, you must make a major investment in the development of people. The breakthrough opportunity lies in merging technology and job design.

Technology is more than automating a particular function. Technology triggers movement in many other programs and processes. It impacts job design; it impacts structure; it impacts compensation. If job design changes, we must also change the way we pay people because our expectations of how they work will change. This, in turn, impacts performance appraisal systems.

Technology should have a major impact on service delivery. In service businesses, there is a difference between quality and service. Quality requires doing the same thing the same way every time. Service requires the flexibility to deal with customers' individual preferences. Often these objectives conflict. The art of management is to achieve both quality and customer satisfaction.

Technology is an opportunity for breakthrough change. Too often, however, automation is not seen as an attempt to make substantial improvements in operation. We need to create breakthrough changes in service delivery, in cost reduction, and in marketing opportunity. How can the information stored in our computers and automated systems help our businesses grow as well as provide differentiation?

American Airlines' Saber system is an excellent example of breakthrough change—one that takes the notion of marketing opportunity to an extreme. The company now makes more money from its computer system than it does from its commercial flights. Insurance companies are also moving beyond their product lines by creating customer files. These files contain information for cross-selling opportunities, market differentiation and niche marketing. While the value of this system is obvious at senior management levels, people in the trenches—in claims, in new business, in underwriting—are often resistant. Their view is that the new system is no better than the old one. If we don't persuade our organization of the system's benefits, we miss an opportunity.

Technological Transformation: The Model

What does a technologically transformed organization look like? (1) It has improved front-line staffing, people who are equipped to satisfy customers' needs. (2) Communication is fluid. (3) Access to data and business information is easy. (4) Technology is a corporate value; PCs can be purchased without the CEO's signature. (5) People investigate and experiment with leading-edge technology.

We must create vertical whole jobs so that people can deliver services, functions and products. To do this, employees must be empowered by the organization, they must have technological tools, and they must have access to information. Beyond this, you can experiment with vertical whole jobs in directions that lead to self-directing and self-managing teams. Once employees are empowered to deliver the whole service to customers, they get involved in other areas—planning their own schedules, setting up their own quality and productivity measures, defining their own goals.

But the horizontal whole job must be in place before employees can take these steps. Let me give you an example. Employees in a model company's money-transfer units have workstations and sophisticated automation; they can access any business in the pipeline at any time. They can then move themselves around from one function to another on the basis of this data. Supervisors don't move stacks of paper from desk to desk; employees do this because they have access to information and are empowered to make changes.

Managing Technological Transformation

The key to managing technological transformation is learning to manage the consequences of events that have not yet occurred. Arranging for someone to pick you up at the airport, for instance, is managing the consequence of a future event. We must anticipate the impact of technological changes and then manage the consequences. If we can imagine these impacts in advance, we will be better prepared to manage them.

Transformation in an organization is the result of a triggering event—a change in legislation, in quality needs, in customer expectations. Senior executives develop a vision for the organization and then evaluate their current state. This defines the gap. Technology's role is to bridge this gap; it is not an end in itself.

Managers mobilize commitment, sell the vision throughout the organization and drive the realization of the vision. For successful change, organizational commitment must extend through every level. Usually organizations that manage change and transformation best are not reacting to crisis. They manage change by creating positive dissatisfaction.

As managers, our job is to be patient and impatient at the same time. We know that change will take time, but we must also prod employees. Get people excited and they will move. Develop a schedule and stick to it. We cannot foresee every angle of the transformation and this will create delays. So build in extra time.

Management Guidelines for Automation

Some guidelines for implementing the first generation of automation include:

Create wide-open communication. People cannot get too much information.

Focus on business objectives—quality, productivity improvements and job enhancement. Don't focus on technology; it is only a tool.

Encourage participation at all levels.

Improve the process before you automate.

Use technicians as facilitators, not decision-makers. Spend time up-front analyzing what you are doing now and planning the future system.

Attend to politics. Determine who the stakeholders are in your technological transformation, understand how they will be affected. Recruit them to your side by creating excitement.

Achieve breakthrough improvement.

In going through a second round of change, remember that change makes people uncomfortable; anticipate renewed resistance. Behave as if you are back at square one. The advantage in round two is that you and your employees already bear the scars from a successful change experience. In a technological transformation, managers can align their energies, talents and skills in the direction of the future. They can work on the system, not in it. They can stop being a crisis intervener and start being a planner. The manager's job is to fuel the system and provide the resources.

Management Guidelines for Transformation

To ensure an effective technological transformation, remember these guidelines:

Involve everyone. Develop all employees' ownership of the design.

Be patient and supportive.

Focus on business objectives of service and quality; then everyone will sign up.

Plan your work.

Sell your vision. Listen as you sell and don't be blinded by your own enthusiasm. Start with the stakeholders and use them to help sell the vision.

Change the system first: Do a work-flow analysis.

Some don'ts:

Don't take the technological aspirin; technology itself is not the solution.

Don't take a corporate line; look at issues from customers' and employees' viewpoints.

Don't allow the system to be staff-driven or, worse, vendor-driven; it must be line-driven.

Don't implement the system prematurely.

Don't fail to include all functions in the transformation; take the broadest view possible and include all pieces of the business in it.

Don't take too long to design a system; any system that takes five years to design will fail because too much will have occurred in the intervening time.

Assembly Line vs. Workstations

Sheila Carvalho
Vice President, Trade Finance
First Bank of Chicago

In 1985, an assembly-line environment prevailed at First Bank of Chicago. Nine people might have been involved in one letter of credit transaction: one person issuing, one amending, one negotiating, one making a payment, one handling files and one typing. Supervisors and second checkers were also involved. This was inefficient and no one saw the end product. We couldn't take advantage of our automated system since it was designed for workstations, not an assembly line. Revenues were declining, expenses were rising, and staff morale and productivity were low. The result: unhappy customers complaining about poor service.

Our trade finance business was at serious risk of closing in 1985 when a new division manager arrived who believed we could reverse this performance. The caveat: We had to make some drastic and very unpopular changes. Our managers had to be prepared for resistance. With the help of management consultants, we embarked on a nine-month reorganization project. Our first mandate was to communicate that these changes were necessary for survival.

Reorganization Begins

Since we wanted to involve all our employees, we conducted a survey among them to identify problems. We formed work groups of non-management employees—people in clerical positions—to define new procedures and to design the work flow. Using a work-effectiveness model, we began to design new jobs.

As a result of this process, the division was split into two production units: an import unit and an export letter of credit unit. Within each unit, we designed whole jobs—one professional handles the product from start to finish. This trade services personnel handles the transaction from issuance through final payment, and works with the customer on a one-to-one basis.

We eliminated clerical positions and supervisory positions. Existing staff was trained for the new professional positions. A six-month mandatory training program was designed that focused on two areas: technical training in processing complete transactions and retraining in the use of the automated system.

Reorganization pushed responsibility and accountability down to the trade services professional level. People in these jobs were well-trained, well-paid and highly motivated. With increased skill levels, each individual took full control of the product and no longer waited for someone in another unit to act before moving the product through. They received one-on-one customer feedback, not just manager feedback. Managers no longer spent time clarifying system procedures or putting out fires between units. Today, problems are resolved at the trade services professional level.

Reorganization was a success. We designed whole jobs, increased pay, and provided job satisfaction. Turnaround time improved dramatically; our objective of a 24-hour turnaround is being met 100 percent. Annual revenues increased by 20-25 percent and profits are up.

Refining the Reorganization

But in 1989, we reorganized again. We needed to keep pace with changes in the marketplace. To stay in the forefront and to grow market share, First National Bank of Chicago needed to develop a new service strategy. At a series of meetings, the entire division staff—production, management, systems, balance and control, and product management—was asked to identify problems created by the reorganization and to work toward their solution. A number of problems surfaced. We had split the division into imports and exports, but this separation of units did not meet customer needs. Work distribution was unbalanced and there were seasonal problems. We had emphasized productivity and neglected the issue of quality. Team spirit was lacking and there was competition between imports and exports, between production and sales. We needed a more cohesive group. Communication between staff and managers was infrequent and inconsistent, leading to confusion and distrust.

Under the 1985 reorganization, the trade services professional was accountable for service to an assigned customer and the salesperson was accountable for revenue. To bridge the gap between production and sales, we created account management teams comprising people from production, sales, product management and systems. Accountability now fell to the team. An account manager position was created and charged with coordinating work flow from sales to production. To create more whole jobs, we integrated the import and export units and cross-trained the staff. Under the recent reorganization, we empowered the account management team to solve internal problems and resolve customer issues. We believe this will generate a more creative environment. By integrating the import and export units, our trade services professionals have more whole jobs, providing greater challenges and growth opportunities. As a result, we expect more open communication. Most important, First National Bank of Chicago will be perceived by both staff and customers as a more responsive organization.

We learned several lessons from our reorganizations. First, you *must* communicate and involve the staff from the beginning of the process. To automate effectively, you must analyze both job design and work flow; system automation alone will fail. Don't emphasize productivity at the expense of quality. Finally, focus on the customer while eliminating internal barriers to excellent customer service.

Management Development at Pepsi-Cola International

John R. Fulkerson, Ph.D.
Director of Human Resources
Pepsi-Cola International

Management development is a fundamental strategy in Pepsi-Cola International's drive to maintain business growth and reputation in the marketplace. As a key player in all of the world's markets, we must have global leaders. We need to develop the kind of talent that enables an executive in Buenos Aires or Singapore to work effectively with a quality manager in New York. To ensure that we have the people who can run the global operation we project for the year 2000, we must leverage the lessons of on-the-job experience in a global environment.

A Bias For Action

We are developing people to work in Pepsi-Cola International's (PCI) fast-paced entrepreneurial culture. Our executives worldwide must have the skills that enable them to analyze a situation and move at a moment's notice, often in conditions of high ambiguity. There is a clear bias for action at PCI; people in the company jokingly say that "*doing* beats thinking about 90 percent of the time." Just be sure you are doing the right thing at the right time.

This bias for action was so strong in the past that we didn't pay as much attention to the development and growth of people as we should have. But to function in a complex global environment, you must pay attention to development. Today's emphasis on the growth, training and development of our employees is a major part of PCI's new corporate values.

In the past, Pepsi-Cola International had a reputation for burning out people. We realized this was not the reputation we wanted nor the way we wished to function. To get where we want to be in the 21st century, we must make sure that people can have a career in our organization. In today's competitive environment, the challenge for us is to recruit and retain top-notch talent.

A Shift Toward Management Development

To help us understand how to select, develop and grow people in international environments, we decided to identify those behaviors and experiences that made people successful at Pepsi-Cola International. If we isolated these factors, we could begin to craft development programs to help people become more effective in the business.

Working with the Center for Creative Leadership, we surveyed a cross-section of people at all levels of the organization, representing different nationalities, cultures and educational backgrounds. We asked respondents to describe the actions of people on-the-job that differentiated the good performers from the bad. Our goal was to obtain enough generic data to help us plan a long-term development program for global executives. We also wanted specific information to help drive Pepsi-Cola International's actions in the short-term.

While analyzing data from the International Success Study, it became clear that factors such as education, age and previous work experience were rather insignificant in a person's success at PCI. The study revealed 12 factors, however, that help executives learn from experience. Each factor has a payoff in business practice.

Identifying Management Success Factors

Managing business complexity is the most critical factor. The executive must be able to do the right thing—look at a problem and formulate the appropriate action. The second most important factor is a *drive-results orientation*. In an international environment, sheer effort sometimes will allow you to succeed. The *ability to lead and manage people of different cultures* is the third factor. Other factors and their payoffs, in order of importance, are:

Executional excellence—Do the right thing right.

Organizational savvy—Teamwork.

Composure under pressure—Maintain focus.

Executive maturity—High integrity.

Technical knowledge—Know the right stuff.

Recruit and develop good people—Leave a legacy.

Positive people skills—Inspire people.

Effective communication—Get the message right.

Impact and influence people—Make a difference.

The survey results don't encompass every element that contributes to success. Factors such as language skills, family adjustment and understanding different cultures also play a role. While managing business complexity is the single most important success element, executives must also demonstrate a broad understanding and adherence to core principles, operating standards, and work ethics in combination with a keen sensitivity to local cultural practices and mores.

We realized that although we had been implementing development, our employees were also learning on their own. Breakthrough development is primarily learning by doing. We also learned that Pepsi-Cola International managers are our basic source for global leadership. These people, typically, are older, more sophisticated, and joined International because they were interested in the global economy and wanted to work in different parts of the world.

Armed with these findings, we decided to craft development assignments that would provide day-to-day experiences to deliver these 12 success factors. Early on, we realized that our selection process was critical and we developed Fast Focus, a selection instrument to help executives identify life-long learners who are most capable of learning from experience.

The 12 success factors are only a departure point for us. When you operate in 150 countries, generalizations about what works in all cultures are difficult to formulate. The survey taught us useful development lessons. First, change occurs so fast that there is no development experience that, in itself, prepares an executive to succeed in a rapidly changing environment. Second, an executive with a broad range of experience will be much better prepared to succeed in this environment.

Pepsi-Cola International is trying to make executives comfortable with the concept of learning from experience. To encourage new ideas, we allow executives to make mistakes. In addition, classroom training is only a small part of our learning mix. If you put people in the right situations, they will learn more from these experiences than they will ever learn in a classroom. This is *breakthrough thinking* in terms of development.

A Feedback Culture

Focused frequent feedback is our most powerful tool. PCI is evolving into a feedback culture. Feedback in all directions is institutionalized. Systems for delivering feedback include instant feedback—our primary path—as well as videotapes and training programs. Annually, every senior manager receives anonymous feedback from peers and subordinates. Coaching, mentoring, accountability-based performance evaluations, inside and outside coursework, and development feedback—where individuals identify the skills they need and we help them get these skills—are other delivery systems.

The glue that holds all this experience together is our comprehensive annual human resources plan. Managers must defend how they expect to grow and develop their employees. The key question here is: What experience does this person need and where can he or she get it? And the plan must be action-driven.

An Experience Matrix

A focus on development raises certain issues. Sometimes it seems the process is ad hoc, has too many transactions, is individually driven and has too little coordination. But *people are having experiences*. We are working to create an experience matrix that defines individual's specific needs and enables us to develop people to their full potential.

The payoff for Pepsi-Cola International is that we have a culture that truly values learning and change. People are becoming empowered. Experience is a part of life, a part of executive growth, not just a program. The career message is that people can stay with us for a long time if they continue to learn. We have developed a more supportive, tolerant environment. In the process, Pepsi-Cola International has become more competitive.

Action Learning: Developing Strategic Leadership at TRW

Andrew J. Kaslow
Director, Management and
Organization Development
TRW, Inc.

According to R. W. Revans, who developed the concept in 1945, *action learning* is "a social process in which managers learn with and from each other by supportive attacks upon real and menacing problems." The main objective of action learning is to learn how to ask questions in conditions of risk. Most training, in contrast, emphasizes finding answers to questions that have been precisely defined by others.

The Action Learning Model

Projects form the core of action learning. The learning model shifts from a classroom focus to a work focus, from a teacher-centered approach to a learner-centered one, from a treatment of hypothetical problems to those that exist in real-time—actual interventions in the mainstream activities of the organization. Revans asserts that companies must be converted into institutions where managers can learn from everyday experiences.

Action learning plays a key role in a TRW manager's development. In the last eight years, several programs were developed at TRW: the strategic management seminar, the advanced management program, and the business leadership program. Sharing a common design, each program consists of two classroom segments, three-to-five days in length, that are separated by a two or three month interim. The first segment is conceptual and oriented toward case studies. During the interim, participants engage in a diagnostic experience as they complete a project. Segment two is data-based and provides executives an opportunity to return to the classroom with what they have learned in the real world. An action plan is the key outcome of this learning experience.

The Strategic Management Seminar

The strategic management seminar was developed from 1983-1986, a period that coincided with the company's transformation from a financially-driven business to one in which strategy became the critical factor. A technology company, TRW was focused inwardly before the transformation and minimally concerned with the outside world. We were engineers who knew what our customers wanted better than they did. Then the world began to change. Globalization became a reality and our customers began to go through a major transformative process, one in which they didn't necessarily want what we had to offer.

This forced TRW to take an outward view of the world—to develop a competitive strategy framework. TRW developed its first seminar in consultation with Michael Porter of the Harvard Business School. Working with division general managers and their direct reports, the first three-day segment focused on case analysis. The interim project had participants return to their businesses and, utilizing the tools that Porter introduced, develop a competitive analysis of their businesses and unit strategic plans. In segment two, these plans were presented and evaluated. There was a real-time application as well—managers presented their business strategies to the CEO.

As a result of the strategic management seminar, we created a common language for strategy development. And there has been significant improvement in business unit plans. But the seminar failed to produce dramatic bottom-line improvement. In the post-1986 period, as TRW experienced a major restructuring, we realized we had many strategic thinkers but few people who understood how to get things done in the organization.

The Advanced Management Seminar

Working with the Harvard Business School from 1987-1989, we designed an action learning experience focused on an organizational process for division vice presidents and general managers. Experts were invited to the first segment of the advanced management seminar to discuss the impact of business systems and information technology on competitive and strategic advantage. We also discussed doing an organizational culture diagnosis. During the interim, executives applied the tools provided by the seminar to analyze the existing structure, systems, culture and human resources management practices. They were to use all available resources, including consultants, to document the current state of their organization and to determine its compatibility with their business strategy. Their assessments were presented in segment two.

In the interim, the Center for Creative Leadership helped us collect leadership data. This was another action learning design in which we generated real information about the organization and about individual issues. In private sessions during segment two, executives received feedback on their leadership competence and skills as well as potential derailment factors.

Using this feedback, executives were to craft an action plan during the second segment. To provide a context for developing their action plans, we told them to focus on two key issues: globalization and TRW's financial environment. TRW has many ex-engineers who don't know much about return on assets, return on equity and other measures of business unit performance.

For a visioning exercise, participants were asked to imagine that it was 1993 and they were reporters for the *Wall Street Journal*. Each executive was to write an article on what he or she, as a transformational leader, had accomplished between 1987-1993. The aim was to move them away from the strategic plan as a blueprint for action to an architectural rendering of how the house would look when completed.

This seminar heightened awareness of the leadership versus management factor in organizational success. It dramatically impacted the behavior of a number of top executives and created significant organizational changes in several key businesses.

The Business Leadership Program

We are launching a business leadership program that centers on quality and customer satisfaction. We are using some of the design developed for the advanced management program because it has been a successful learning experience. Our functional, high-potential people will participate in this program and report directly to general managers from the advanced management seminar. After segment one, these high-potentials will work on an interim program that measures internal and external customer satisfaction. The second segment will focus on an action plan that improves customer satisfaction through continuous improvement.

We anticipate several outcomes from this program: It should broaden the outlook of our functional high-potentials; it should lead to specific improvements in organizational effectiveness, particularly in terms of quality; and it should enhance the individuals' development planning process. As a by-product, the program offers an effective way of getting to know people in TRW. Those involved in succession planning and executive development will get a rich set of data points about these individuals as we work with them on specific projects for one or two weeks. This gives us a rare opportunity to watch people as they interact with their colleagues and deal analytically with business problems.

Action learning—one element in our multifaceted approach to executive development—is a powerful tool for individual and organization development. It is one that requires top level commitment and support. Accordingly, TRW's key executives are presenters and faculty in the action learning programs.

Transforming Managers At Texaco

Richard C. Conant

Manager, Human Resources Development
Texaco Inc.

With the slogans, "We Are Going to Thrive, Not Just Survive," and "Texaco is Ours to Build," the once highly respected Texaco began its recovery from the dark days of 1985-1988 with the rebuilding of its corporate management style and corporate culture.

Texaco recognized the key role middle managers play, from first-line supervisors to general managers. In a transformation, you quickly capture senior management—they always have stockholders and boards of directors at their backs—and you easily capture the workers because they have paid dearly for the lack of change. But middle management feel threatened and don't want to change. You must capture middle management, however, or they will kill your effort.

Transformation Through Awareness Training

We implemented awareness-training classes to support the transformation of Texaco's management behavior from an autocratic style that had dominated the company for 50 years. By changing our management behavior to an open style, we hoped to empower employees who would then become responsible for their businesses at Texaco.

To understand why "Texaco is Ours to Build" was the theme introduced in the awareness classes, you must recall certain events from 1984-1989. In that period, our employees (at the time, 52,000; soon to be 78,000; and then reduced to 26,000) went from the elation and pride of a major oil company acquisition, Getty Oil, to the confusing and embarrassing acknowledgment of a Chapter 11 bankruptcy. Some of the results: a legal settlement of over $3 billion; a major restructuring of the company; and the sale of some of our most valuable assets.

Texaco was a major oil company with only seven years supply of underground reserves. We couldn't find oil as fast as we were using it. In characteristic autocratic style, the then-CEO doubled our reserves with a dramatic business strategy. In one $10.1 billion purchase, he bought Getty Oil, doubled our reserves and quadrupled Texaco's life. We faced extraordinary problems after this transaction. Texaco eventually faced the largest legal judgment ever against an American corporation—$10.1 billion in favor of Pennzoil. We filed Chapter 11 bankruptcy to protect our assets. Then Texaco paid the largest settlement ever against a judgment—$3.1 billion.

Jim Kinnear, Texaco's CEO, arrived on the scene just in time, in January 1987. He faced serious issues. He was responsible for actually declaring bankruptcy in April 1987. He knew we couldn't fight off the creditors until we restructured, sold assets, raised money and paid off our debt. He sold prize assets to raise the money. Shareholders were upset because dividends weren't paid for two years. Yet, most remained loyal.

The CEO's Vision

Employees were worried; they were concerned about whether they would have jobs or not. We were approaching the teachable moment. Within the first month, Kinnear made the first of many speeches to employees. In that speech, he said, "Texaco is ours to build." He held out hope.

Kinnear said that we must shape a vision, a mission; senior management must direct Texaco or it would get lost. His vision was for Texaco to become one of the most admired corporations in the world—as well as its leading oil company. The greatest loss in the lawsuit wasn't money but people's trust in Texaco. Texaco's theme had been trust; this had to be recaptured.

To rebuild a great company, Kinnear knew he needed people who were devoted to the company and customers who wanted to do business with them. He underlined these objectives, among others:

High-quality products

Fair return

Inspired leadership

A record of productivity and profits

Participation

The core words in his first speech were: destiny; public approval; fire in the belly; responsibility; getting control; identifying customers—in essence, *do it now*. Pyramidal organizations don't understand "do it now." They wait for instructions about how to do it.

The Teachable Moment

The issue for the training and development group was how to teach these concepts. How do you tell managers who are scared that the teachable moment is here. They know they must do something different, but what? We told them to empower people, to listen to employees.

Managers learn to manage by watching others manage. Managers also draw from their own personality style. But we can never change a manager unless we create a teachable moment. However, the manager must believe the moment has come. It is usually forced by outside competition. Xerox, for instance, was the copy-company of the world until the Japanese emerged. Xerox changed so the company could survive. Ford Motor Company did the same. Frequently, the second impetus is an attempted hostile takeover or a lawsuit. A third way to force culture change is to oust top management and install a new regime.

Managers are behavior-driven and inevitably will swing to the new management system. Whatever the path, managers must be honest with employees. With all the right elements in place, and sustained over a period of time, you have an opportunity to make change. It takes a long time. In certain areas there is immediate understanding of the new values; some people grasp them right away. Others will never change. We get discouraged. But we know now that the new culture is planted. There are managers at Texaco today who operate in a style that couldn't have been imagined in 1984. This will grow. Unless you have top management's long-term support, don't begin this journey. If they abandon you after the process begins, you will hurt many people.

Beginning the Culture Transformation

Hogan T. McWilliams

Manager, Training
Texaco Inc.

Our approach to the "Texaco is Ours to Build" Conference was revolutionary for us. We held a three-day conference. Most of the moderators' input occurred in the first day. The second two days were largely self-managed time. Our participants were accustomed to considerable structure. In this case, however, they walked into a room and found a circle of chairs. In the middle of the circle was a table with a box covered by black cloth. People were uncomfortable; this was strange stuff in Texaco's old culture.

Without any introduction, the moderator played a tape of Jim Kinnear's speech at Texaco in 1987. After listening to the tape, we asked attendees to name the most important things Kinnear said to them. We also asked them what personal barrier would inhibit them from buying Kinnear's vision. We unveiled a box in the middle of the table and asked everyone to bury their barriers—symbolically. We asked people to step up to the box, read their answers and bury them in the box. About one-third of the group seriously examined themselves to answer this question. The rest were just "playing along" at this point.

After a break, the room was rearranged in a more conventional style. We explained that Texaco was at the bottom of the well. Then we discussed transformation and quantum leaps. We talked about addiction to rules and the comfort of the standard operating manual. People became nervous when we discussed the possibility of doing away with manuals.

Teaching the Vision

Vision was the centerpiece of this effort. Keep in mind that vision was foreign to our company in 1987. In this connection, we explored imaging. We found that picturing the idea of successful outcomes can be powerful. We also engaged in the *peak experience*, a sensory-

memory exercise with past successes. Many people thought all this was too much like *Twilight Zone*; some people bought it; but most were skeptical.

As we closed day one, we talked about issues that were more acceptable to traditional business people: the differences between efficiency and effectiveness, for instance. Peter Drucker says that there is nothing so useless as doing with great efficiency that which should not be done at all. And we talked about the differences between urgent and important things. We ended the first day by asking people to design a personal vision for their part of the company.

On day two, we examined about 10 models that reinforced our vision theme. We arranged small group discussions and, in the afternoon, we set aside time for participants to work on their individual visions. We departed from our norm at conferences and provided self-managed time. Those who had been incredulous at the end of the first day were now beginning to shift their attitudes.

On day three, conferees invited top executives from their departments to attend the symposium; the executives were asked to listen to their employees' visions. Some executives were ready to embrace what their subordinates presented; others were not. Some managers readily endorsed the visions; others gave tacit approval; the latter truly didn't understand this process because it was alien to Texaco's culture. We concluded the conference by reassembling people in a circle and asking them what they had learned. Some who were skeptical at the outset now championed the process.

There was no formal conference evaluation: We distributed blank pieces of paper and asked people to write whatever they wanted about their experience. Some people were encouraged about Texaco's new leadership, felt they could be a part of it and could make a difference; some said that this direction provided hope;

some felt challenged and empowered to make change in the company, and that success was their personal responsibility.

Lessons Learned

We ran this training conference for about two years and over 700 top and middle-level managers participated. We learned that change is not easy. We slide back now and then. Some people grumble. Not everyone is on board. But our culture is changing from the highly structured model it once was.

Texaco will apply for the Baldrige Award in 1992. Announcing that we will compete for this award is it-self a counter-cultural statement for Texaco. Among the criteria for this award are visionary leadership, team-work, customer rapport and satisfaction, and supplier partnerships. We are not there yet, but this is where we are headed.

We are on a journey with no end in sight. We have learned, first, that you don't attempt such a journey without a total commitment to the ideas. It is a long-term process. Second, the human spirit is boundless. It is a renewable source of energy that cannot be harnessed without destroying people's enthusiasm. This spirit must be set loose. Traditional management styles control the human spirit. We must shift from control to release and empowerment.

Creating Intrapreneurs

Carolyn D. Holt

Senior Consultant
Union Carbide Chemicals and
Plastics Company, Inc.

The 1980s saw unprecedented change in American business as corporations sought non-traditional ways to become competitive in the new global marketplace. To survive in today's competitive, rapidly changing environment, organizations must be able to create and sustain cultures that encourage and nurture innovation and the entrepreneurial spirit.

The Innovation Challenge

Gifford Pinchot, whose theories on intrapreneuring have had a significant impact on new business development, emphasizes the challenge posed to major corporations: Innovate for survival. How can American industry meet the innovation challenge? Pinchot emphasizes that the corporation needs the innovation and the initiative of the entrepreneur, and the entrepreneur needs the resources of the corporation. The problem is that while corporations need intrapreneurship, they aren't designed to encourage and reward it. Bureaucracy and control systems support the status quo and block innovation. Corporations must learn to create the entrepreneurial business culture necessary for successful internal venturing or intrapreneuring will fail. Intrapreneuring must be approached from a systems perspective. Organizations are systems composed of interrelated parts. Any attempt to change one part of the organization—to start a new venture, for example—impacts other parts of the organization. Another characteristic of organizations is resistance to change. Organizations, like water, choose the path of least resistance. If something happens to upset the system's balance, the system will push back to maintain the status quo.

In addition to the challenges of the global market, Union Carbide experienced a number of setbacks in the 1980s. After the Bhopal tragedy, its stock fell and GAF attempted a takeover. The company survived by selling important and profitable businesses and by incurring huge debt. Union Carbide restructured and emerged a smaller, highly leveraged corporation with a mission and sense of purpose. To survive and grow, new business development became a high priority goal. The Chemicals and Plastics business group developed a vision of the future that included the goal of creating 30 new businesses, each with about $50 million in sales, by the year 2000.

The Specialty Chemicals Division has a significant role in meeting this challenge. Recently, the division has experienced success in implementing an intrapreneuring program and in creating a culture focused on new business development. Identifiable success factors and replicable steps emerged that have valuable implications for other corporations.

The Specialty Chemicals Division has created three new businesses through its intrapreneuring program: one venture team uses technology to enhance the delivery of therapeutic products for the skin and hair; another team developed a business that enables Union Carbide to safely and efficiently send out chemical samples in small packages; and a third team, which just became a formal subsidiary, uses chemicals to restore and preserve marble floors. These initial results—achieved within a short time frame of less than nine months—also effected culture change. Intrapreneuring created the culture necessary for achieving the division's core value of *Innovation for Growth*.

Critical Leverage Points for Intrapreneuring

Based on this division's experience, it is clear that certain levers are critical in making culture change happen. These levers carry the acronym VAST, which sums up the immensity of the change required to create organizational culture that supports new business development.

V stands for Volunteerism. Rather than selecting people to innovate, volunteerism enabled 117 enthusiastic people to come forward.

A stands for Attention from senior management. Senior managers must communicate that new business development, innovation and growth are critical to the organization's survival and success. This is the most important lever.

S stands for a trilogy of senior management responsibilities—Strategic direction, Structure and Sponsorship. Senior managers must provide a clear vision, identify areas for new ventures and specify criteria for selecting and evaluating ventures; they must build a non-bureaucratic organizational structure; they must model the championship of new ventures and reward sponsorship of new business development.

T stands for Training of teams and sponsors. Teams are trained to develop sound business plans; sponsors are trained to champion new ventures.

Steps for Implementation of Intrapreneuring

Although the specific actions that can be taken to utilize these levers will vary from one organization to another, eight generic steps are replicable:

(1) *Setting Direction.* Senior management must define the organization's vision and values, the strategic business direction, areas and criteria for new ventures, and then communicate this across the organization. In the Specialty Chemicals Division, this led to articulation of its core value: Innovation for Growth. The management team was continuously involved in communicating this core value. Senior executives visited all 13 division sites and conducted half-day workshops. Workshops emphasized how Innovation for Growth would be translated into action—by championing new products and services, for instance, and assuming risks in the market. These workshops helped executives identify factors that inhibited change. Most important, the workshops provided powerful evidence of management attention.

(2) *Diagnosing the Organization.* This can be done in formal or informal ways. In Specialty Chemicals, diagnosis began informally with the senior management team's observations and discussions in the workshops as well as elsewhere. There was also an audit—in the form of a 24-part questionnaire designed and evaluated by Pinchot and Company—which identified factors that supported and hindered innovation in the division. The

results led to the decision to pursue intrapreneuring as the method for new business development.

(3) *Structuring the Organization.* Senior managers must build a structure that supports new business development, minimizes bureaucracy and assigns accountability.

(4) *Developing Business Concepts.* Next, possible areas for new business development should be identified. Three carefully selected ad hoc groups of divisional managers developed more than 20 general areas at Union Carbide.

(5) *Calling for Volunteers.* Self-nomination is a key to success. Intrapreneurs can't be convinced to become passionately committed to an idea. The call at Specialty Chemicals uncovered 117 enthusiastic innovators and leaders representing all functions, locations and job levels. The invitation letter stated that people were needed to create new businesses through internal venture teams; the opportunity areas were included; and it noted that not all proposed ventures would be funded.

(6) *Training for Intrapreneurs and Sponsors.* Pinchot and Company ran the first "school for intrapreneurs." It consisted of three two-day workshops, several months apart. The first workshop introduced concepts, reviewed the division's growth mission and the criteria to be used for selecting ventures, and business planning. By the end of this session, 17 teams were formed. At the second workshop, each team presented its plan and received feedback from the consulting company. Between the second and third meeting, each team recruited a sponsor—a senior manager who would champion its venture. At the third workshop, each team presented its business plan to a group of venture capitalists who provided candid, objective feedback.

Training for sponsors is a must to gain middle management support for intrapreneuring. Senior management convened a division-wide workshop that included 85 middle managers to provide an overview of the critical role of the sponsor. The division president laid out his expectation that all managers would support the effort "or get out of the way."

(7) *Commissioning Ventures and Contracting with Teams.* Managers must decide which ventures to fund and must provide a reward system. Venture approval means that most of the team will work full-time on the venture. In Specialty Chemicals, the reward system simulated the external environment for entrepreneurs: If the venture succeeded, teams could earn considerable money. There was a safety net, however, which allowed participants to return to a comparable job if the venture failed for reasons other than incompetence.

(8) *Starting up Venture Teams.* Teams face start-up issues and benefit from working on a group process.

Among other issues, they must identify their collective vision of success and milestones for measuring such success. They must define accountability and standard operating procedures, and decide how they want to work together.

Unfinished Business

The eight replicable steps, which involve multiple, congruent levers for organization change, resulted in the creation of an enabling environment for new business development within the division. Despite the initial success, internal venturing alone will not allow the division to achieve Innovation for Growth. Management will use other strategies as well, such as acquisitions, joint ventures and strategic partnerships. But a culture that fosters new business development has been created. The organizational culture is now ready to implement successful external business development strategies. The organization is beginning to understand how much change and challenge is required to achieve Innovation for Growth.

DATE DUE

DEMCO NO. 38-298